See You on the Field

See You on the Field

Jeff Crume

JEFF CRUME
MINISTRIES

Dedication

Linfield Lions
Middle School Flag Football Team

Contents

Forward

Would you be interested in coaching Flag Football this season, we're short on coaches, and I could really use some help? The voice of Mr. John Broussard, Athletic Director for Linfield Christian Middle School, resounded over the morning-time hustle and bustle of the Linfield Middle School campus.

"I really don't think I can...but if you can't find anyone else, let me know," I quickly responded. As I walked away I suddenly got a flash of all the times as a Pastor I asked someone for their help at the church and they would tell me, "Pastor, I really don't think I can, but if you can't find anyone else, let me know."

I knew instantly that the Lord was dealing with me about coaching. "Don't turn around," I said to myself, "Just get in your car and drive away." The more I tried convincing myself of all the reasons why I couldn't coach, the more I knew I was supposed to.

"Mr. Broussard, I feel like I'm supposed to coach." Before I knew it, I found myself back in front of Mr. Broussard volunteering to coach flag football. Little did I know my life was about to change forever.

"See You on the Field" is a treasury of the ideas, insights, and lessons of life I shared with my players and their families during the season. Even though this book is written to the Linfield Lion's Flag Football team, the insights and principles of life will inspire and develop the champion in anyone who reads it.

Whether it's game strategies, life lessons, or the play-by-play game recaps, "See You on the Field" will inspire, encourage, and challenge the champion in you. "See You on the Field" is also a great tool for coaches, parents, athletes and those who desire to become, or inspire others to become, all they can possibly be.

By the way, coaching is the greatest way to make a lasting impression in the lives of young people. Never pass up an opportunity to coach. Resist the urge to "wait to see if anyone else can do it."

*Never pass up an opportunity
to make an investment in
someone else's life.*
- Jeff Crume

See You on the Field
...of Life

Dear Linfield Lions,

Congratulations on finishing what you started. It seems like it's been forever since that first day of tryouts, and here you are at the end of the season.

If you look back you will see that not only did you make the team, not only did you make it through the entire season, but you achieved a goal! You set out to be on the football team and you made it. Not only did you make the football team, you have learned a lot! You've learned a lot about football, about life and about yourself.

Football and Life both are about learning and growing. You can't learn the entire football playbook in a day, and you won't learn the Playbook of Life in a day either. It takes time, in fact, a lifetime.

I wanted to leave you a gift; something that you could open not just once, but for a lifetime. On the following pages are a collection of the ideas, practices, insights, life lessons, principles and seeds of life that have been sown into you during this season.

I believe they have fallen on good soil and will produce a great harvest in your life. Thank you for allowing me the privilege of being your coach.

I believe in you!

See you on the field of life

~ Coach Crume

Tryouts

Introductions & Expectations

INTRODUCTIONS

I count it an honor and privilege to be your coach this year. Welcome to Flag Football and Life. You are about to embark on the most exciting, the most demanding, and most rewarding time of your life.

During this season you will learn skills and principles, that, if received and applied, will produce in you greatness; a true champion in Football and in Life.

Principle 1: *The Greeting*

The way you address or greet someone says a lot about you. Teach yourself to address or greet your coaches, your teachers, those in authority, or your elders by, "Mr." or "Mrs." and their last name.

Use, "Ma'am," or "Sir," when speaking with people in authority. It will set you above the crowd.

Principle 2: *Handshake with Eye Contact*

When you greet someone for the first time, extend your right hand confidently and grip the person's hand whom you are greeting firmly.

Without inflicting pain, shake the person's hand firmly a few times up and down, and looking him or her right in the eyes introduce yourself with confidence. "Hello Mr. Broussard, my name is Jeff Crume."

Say the person's name and your name with firmness and confidence; it's a great sign of respect for both the person you are greeting and yourself.

Using someone's last name when you greet him or her is a sign of respect. Respect is the foundation that champions and successful people build their lives on.

Principle 3: *Respect*

The first lesson in Football and Life is to be respectful. *Respect is the greatest key to success both on and off the field.* Respect lays the foundation and sets the boundaries for successful relationships, and both football and life are about building successful relationships.

EXPECTATIONS

Football and Life, without expectations, leads to failure. To expect means to anticipate or look forward to the coming or occurrence of. Live life and play football with expectancy.

Expect to win. You won't always win, but expect to! Every time you walk on to that football field you should expect to win. Every day you get out of bed and you are breathing, you should expect to win.

Expect to learn. Each game and each day of life is filled with opportunities and possibilities brilliantly disguised as problems and challenges. Your job is to embrace every play, every day, expecting to learn. Use each day, each opportunity that comes your way to learn.

Remember: *Learners become leaders*

Expect good things to happen. Expectation is a powerful life-force that catapults you to your destiny. See yourself successful. See yourself winning. See yourself learning and becoming all you desire to be. Each day expect good things to happen to you.

Expectation to Succeed Attracts Success!

Success in the game of football and in life requires dedication, attitude, sportsmanship, and ability; all of which will be required of you both on and off the field.

Now is the time for you decide if flag football is for you and if you are for flag football. Now is the time for you to determine that you are for life and life is for you.

Accountability

You will be held accountable if you commit to the game of football. If you commit to life, you will be held accountable. We are all accountable to someone.

Accountability Produces Champions

When you give someone permission to hold you accountable, it proves that you are serious. You could just skate through life and see what happens, or you could determine today that you are going to make life the best it can be, for you and for others around you

Your mission, should you choose to accept it, for the game of Football and in Life is...

1. Be Dependable—Football and Life are team sports. Your team is counting on you. Say what you mean and mean what you say. If you give your word, keep it.

2. Be Prompt—Late players don't play. Promptness is a sign of selflessness. Selflessness produces winners both on and off the field.

3. Be Respectful—Respect your coaches, your parents, your school, your team, your opponent and yourself.

4. Be Informed—"I didn't know" is not an excuse. It is your responsibility to find out the information that's important to you and your team. Know the rules. Know what's expected of you. Ignorance is not bliss. Ignorance is not acceptable in the life of a winner.

5. Be Your Best—Leave it *ALL* on the field. Both Football and Life will require everything you have, and then some.

Decide today to be your best at whatever you do. Be the best wide receiver, quarterback, center, rusher, student, son, daughter, or friend. *Whatever you chose to do, be the best you that you can possibly be.*

*Football and Life require everything
you have; and then some.*
- Coach Crume

Winning & Losing

Winning and Losing is an Attitude, not a Result

Winning and Losing

Winning and losing is an attitude, not a result. In Football and in Life there will be times when you win and times when you lose, but make sure and guard yourself from becoming your results.

Winners lose and losers win. Winning doesn't necessarily make you a winner and losing doesn't necessarily make you a loser. Who you are determines your results, your results don't determine who you are.

Winners win and lose with the right attitude. Winners celebrate their victories AND their losses. Winners look at losing as an opportunity to discover what didn't work.

Remember: *Losing is an opportunity to find out what didn't work.*

Discipline

Discipline is the ability to make yourself do the things that you don't want to do, but must do in order to succeed. Self-discipline is the greatest discipline in life and sports. At all cost, develop self-discipline.

There are two pains you will face in life—the pain of discipline or the pain of regret. The pain of discipline weighs ounces, the pain of regret weighs tons. Discipline says, "I'm glad I did." Regret says, "I wish I would have." (Jim Rohn)

Remember: *A lazy man aims at nothing and hits it 100% of the time.*

The only secret to success is WORK! Winners never quit and quitters never win.

When the Going Gets Tough

Dear Team,

I'm certain that by now some of you are asking yourself why you ever signed up for Flag Football in the first place. Some of you are frustrated, tired, and sore. Some are even wondering if you should just quit.

If you are feeling any of those things, let me encourage you that you are right where you are supposed to be. You are in the right place!

In case you are wondering what you got yourself into, in case you may be one of those trying to decide if flag football was such a good idea after all, I wanted to take a minute to remind you of what you've learned so far. *So far you have learned:*

RESPECT

Respect is *a high or special regard or value for something or someone.* So far you have learned to respect your coach, each other, your parents and teachers, and yourself. You've learned that you have value and that your value makes this team more valuable.

Remember: *Respect is not demanded or deserved, it is earned, both on and off the field.*

EXPECTATION

You've learned that Football and Life *expect* something of you. You can't just show up on the field and do whatever you want to do or whatever feels good to you at the time.

You have learned that both Football and Life take *work* and that you need to be *dependable, prompt, respectful, informed,* and to always be *your best.*

WINNING

You've learned that winning is an attitude, not an identity. Winners lose and losers win. Winning is an opportunity to celebrate what you did right. Losing is the opportunity to find out what you did wrong and correct it.

DISCIPLINE

You've learned that both Football and Life require you to have discipline. Discipline is the ability to make yourself do the things you don't want to do, but must do, in order to succeed.

Remember: *A lazy man aims at nothing and hits it 100% of the time.*

PAY ATTENTION & FOLLOW INSTRUCTIONS

You've learned that both Football and Life require you to pay attention and follow instructions. You've learned that the football, just like life, comes at you fast, and sometimes unexpected. You've also learned that the price of not paying attention is sometimes pain.

Remember: *The more we pay attention and the more we follow instruction, the more successful we are both on and off the field.*

PURPOSE

You've learned that both Football and Life require you to be on purpose. Study with purpose, run with purpose, pass and receive the football with purpose, play with purpose, and even walk on the field with purpose.

Purpose is a determination to act in a certain way. Purpose is knowing what you are doing, and why you are doing it.

Remember: *Whatever your hand finds to do, do it with all your might.*

No Superstars

We've learned that there are no *superstars*. The greatest star is the one you help make someone else become.

> **Matthew 18:1-4** "When asked who is the greatest in the kingdom of Heaven, Jesus called a little child unto him, and set him in the middle of the crowd and said, "Verily I say unto you, Except you be converted, and become as a little children, you shall not enter into the kingdom of heaven. Whosoever therefore shall humble himself as this little child, the same is greatest in the kingdom of heaven."

Remember: *The way you shine is by helping someone else shine.*

Teamwork

One of the most physically challenging lessons we've learned so far is teamwork. You were tied to the person beside you and had to learn how to work together.

You learned that a team works together at all times to achieve the same common goal. You learned that there is no "I" in team. You learned to value everyone on the team.

You learned that even if you can't throw the farthest or run the fastest, you are still a valuable part of this team. You learned that your gift is not just for yourself, but to help others become the best they can be.

Remember: *Together Everyone Achieves More*

I know many of you are feeling the effects of a hard couple of weeks of practice. You have had some good times and some not-so-good times. But if you read over the things you have learned so far really believe they are important to your life and future, *I strongly recommend* you finish the journey you have started.

FINAL THOUGHT: *A Divided Kingdom*

Jesus taught the greatest lesson of all for a flag football team in Matthew 12:25 when He said, "…every kingdom divided against itself is brought to desolation; and every city or house divided against itself shall not stand."

You have to decide what you do, but whatever you decide, make your decision and stick with it. Don't allow yourself to be divided; one minute you like being on the team, the next minute when it gets hard you don't like it. Whatever you decide, stick with it until the very end!

Remember: *When the going gets tough, the tough get going.*

I believe in you!

See You on the Field!

~ Coach Crume

Whatever you decide to do,
stick with it until the very end.
- Coach Crume

Life Lessons

ASSIGNMENT OF TEAMS

Today we split the team in to three separate teams: Team "Alpha," Team "Omega," and Team "David." For clarification, each player for each team is assigned an offensive and defensive position. Some players have more than one position by their name indicating they can play multiple positions on that team.

Life Lesson—*In life, learn how to play multiple positions. The more problems you solve, the more valuable you are. The more diverse you become, the more valuable you are.*

During a game, each team will have the potential of playing both offense and defense. Team "David" will be the team we play when we are up against the strongest or "Giant" of opponents.

"Alternates" are additional players that we will substitute in when Team David is on the field. Also, as a reminder, everyone should always be ready all the time. You never know when you may be called on.

TEAM CAPTAINS

We assigned team captains for both offense and defense. Remember that Team Captains are the only players on the field that communicate with the referees during a game. Also remember that Team Captain Positions are *earned*, not *deserved*.

We expect captains to maintain a standard of excellence and leadership throughout the entire season both on and off the field.

Life Lesson—*Nothing is free in life. Life doesn't owe you anything. The price of all success is effort. The more effort, the more success.*

Sportsmanship

Sportsmanship is defined as, "Conduct considered fitting for a sports person, including observance of the rules of fair play, respect for others, and graciousness in losing."

Good Sportsmanship is expected every time we are on the field. We demonstrate sportsmanship in the following key areas:

Take A Knee—Taking a knee is a form of respect, for our coaches, those in authority who are speaking to us, and for other players who may get injured on the field.

As a team, when we are given instruction to "Take A Knee" we will all come together and put our **left knee** to the ground with our right knee up and our hands on our right knee.

We will not be slouched or sitting on our bottoms, but upright, giving respect and our attention to whoever is talking. In the case of an injured player, we will take a knee for as long as the player is "down" on the field.

Substitution

Substitution is when a player who is waiting on the sidelines is sent in to relieve another player on the field. As a team, when a substitution is called for, both the player going into the game and the player coming out of the game is expected to "hustle" on and off the field.

No slouching, walking or shuffling; but hustling! High fives, "hoorahs" and any other forms of encouragement for one another by the two players is totally acceptable!

Disappointment

Disappointment is being dissatisfied, unhappy, or frustrated with something or someone. It's perfectly ok to be disappointed, but as a team we will not be boisterous, rude or disrespectful in our expression.

In other words, we won't let the world know how we feel. One of the Fruits of the Spirit is "Self-Control" and we will demonstrate *Self-Control* to the best of our ability at all times.

When the referee makes a call that we don't agree with, we will refrain from vocalizing or showing our frustration. We will accept the consequence and move our team forward.

As a player, when we don't make the play we wanted to make or do our best on a play, or when one of our teammates doesn't do his or her best, we will refrain from vocalizing our frustration with our team or with ourselves.

Be a voice of encouragement to others and to yourself at all times.

Life Lesson—*Disappointment*

I know we already addressed disappointment in an earlier section, but I felt led to address it again as today's Life Lesson.

I want to encourage you that Life can be disappointing at times. In fact, Life is filled with disappointment. Sometimes you win and sometimes you lose. Sometimes you pass a test and sometimes you fail. Sometimes you get picked and sometimes you don't.

Sometimes you can try your hardest at something and it just doesn't work out the way you planned. There are even times in life when you spend all your time and effort preparing to do a certain thing, and Life throws you a curve ball and you end up having to do something else.

Find comfort in **Psalm 37:23** that says, "The steps of a good man are ordered by the LORD: and he delighteth in his way."

When we don't get the position on the football team, or in life, that we think we should, let's trust that *The One* who orders our steps knows what He is doing, and that He would never do anything to cause us harm.

I Believe In You!

See You on the Field!

~ Coach Crume

Sometimes you get picked,
and sometimes you don't.
- Coach Crume

What's in the Water?

We used to have a saying, "what's in the water today?" to describe an exceptionally difficult day. Not just difficult, but out of the ordinary. "What's in the water today?" meant that everything and everybody just seemed to be "out of sorts."

Well, I must say, "Something was in the water today!" Today had to be the most frustrating of all days we have had on the field as a team. While I must admit some were "on your game," others, including those who should be leaders, were just flat out "squirrely."

I couldn't seem to keep your attention for more than five minutes, and most of you seemed to want to give instruction rather than follow it. Some of our best running backs and receivers were goofing off with each other or your QBs, or running three quarters the way down the field when we called the play dead and gave instructions to get back to the line of scrimmage.

Even when I attempted to gather us together and share valuable Life Lessons regarding self-discipline and self-control, some were laughing, snickering, and seemed to have more interest in what your neighbor was saying, or what the cheerleaders were doing, than what I was trying to share.

Now I know we had our fair share of distractions today, but I saw behavior today in some of you that shocked me, because that is just not you! You are better than that!

WHAT WILL YOU BE?

Statistics say only 10% of you will become anyone of significance in this world. Some statistics say 25% of you will flat-out fail at life period, while the rest of you fall in the middle somewhere; not significant, but not insignificant. Well, *I refuse to believe that about any of you!*

I believe in you! I believe you were created for greatness and that you have what this team, and this world, needs!

I would not be a Coach, a good Coach, if I only patted you on the back and never disciplined or "chastened" you when you get off track or out of line. Hebrews 12:6 says, "For whom the Lord loveth he chasteneth."

My Conclusion

I've been praying about today since we left practice, and I have come to the conclusion that today was not a *crisis*, it was not an "act of rebellion," but simply a temporary memory lapse—A momentary lapse of memory of who we are and what we stand for as Linfield Christian Middle School Athletes!

So I took the liberty to put together on the next page a reminder of who you are, so that you can look yourself in the mirror, make the necessary adjustments and get your self back on track! (Print this list and stick it on your mirror and read it three times a day)

I AM...

1. A Child of God (Romans 8:16)

2. Included (Ephesians 1:13)

3. Redeemed (Psalm 107:2)

4. Forgiven (Colossians 1:13, 14)

5. Justified (Romans 5:1)

6. Blessed (Ephesians 1:3)

7. A New Creature (2 Corinthians 5:17)

8. Chosen before the creation of the world (Eph. 1:4, 11)

9. A Partaker of God's Divine Nature (II Peter 1:4)

10. A Son (or Daughter) of God (Romans 8:14)

11. Above only and not beneath (Deuteronomy 28:13)

12. The Head and not the tail (Deuteronomy 28:13)

13. An Heir of God and Joint Heir with Jesus (Rom. 8:17)

14. Strong in the Lord (Eph. 6:10)

15. Blessed coming in and blessed going out (Deut. 28:6)

16. More than a conqueror (Romans 8:37)

17. An imitator of Jesus (Ephesians 5:1)

18. Salt and light of the earth (Matthew 5:13-14)

19. An Heir of eternal life (1 John 5:11, 12)

20. A Linfield Lion!

Let the Games Begin

"The Thrill of Victory"

Temecula Prep
14-12 - Linfield Lions

Game Recap—*The Thrill of Victory*

(Coach Payne)

The Lions got off to a rough start on offense resulting in the defense being backed against the goal line on several opening series.

The defense embraced the challenge, making several goal-line stands and keeping us in the game. While the entire defense proved to be incredibly stout, Justin Locke was one of the early stars making 2 touchdown saving tackles in the early going. The defense also adapted well despite some equipment challenges involving Temecula Preps flags that refused to come lose with one, two–sometimes three attempts!

Another defensive star, John Henry, turned the tide in the first half with an interception deep in Patriot territory. John's interception led to the Lion's first score of the season and turned the momentum of the game.

Eldon Meacham also made an open field, touchdown-saving tackle. Josh Brunell and Connor Kostecka combined to force a Patriot fumble.

Once the offense settled in, they took charge of the game. Kobe Daludado was Lion's leading rusher and receiver totaling more than 90 yards in combined yardage including a 45 yard touchdown run where he knifed through the Patriots defense eluding at least 5 attempted tackles.

The game's deciding play turned out to be a 10 yard pass from Quarterback Mitchell Foster to Caleb Smeraldi to complete a 2-point conversion, giving the Lions their first lead of the game, in what turned out to be the winning margin 14-12.

Santa Rosa A

"The Agony of Defeat"

Santa Rosa A
36-0 – Santa Rosa "A"

Taking a line from Coach Payne's recap, the Linfield Lions have now experienced the "thrill of victory," and the "agony of defeat."

Yesterday's game proved to be one of our biggest challenges yet. Despite our loss, we had another chance to put to practice what we know, and discover a lot of what we don't know. One thing we didn't know was how we would play "under extreme pressure." Every time we tried to move the ball forward we were shut down.

Remember: *Pressure is the greatest test of skill and nature*

PRESSURE

Pressure can cause us to do the right thing or the wrong thing. Pressure can bring out both the best and worse in us, and yesterday we experienced both. For some, the pressure of a bigger, faster and more experienced team caused frustration, anger, and mistakes. For others, that same pressure created determination in them to try harder.

The key to being a champion is learning how to use what is meant to defeat you to motivate you to reach higher, go further, and be stronger.

Pressure also reveals our weaknesses. If we know what we are weak in, we can go to work on strengthening that area.

Remember: "Greater is He that is in you than he that is in the world!" (1 John 4:4)

NEW OFFENSIVE STRATEGY

In Football and in Life, sometime you have to try different strategies. Someone once said that *stupidity is doing the same thing and expecting difference results*. In life, if things are working, don't get discouraged, make adjustments.

In the next game, Centers and Guards will run straight out 5-7-yard button hook patterns, putting you between the defensive rusher and the QB. We cannot block the rusher, but we can run patterns that put ourselves between the rusher and our QB, giving our QB the opportunity to throw to us, or buy time for him to hit another receiver down field.

Receivers will run quick 5-7 yard down-and-out, down-and-in, and slant patterns. We need quick, short patterns that help us move the ball and gain yardage quickly.

Remember: *Three downs to get a first down, three more downs to get a touchdown.*

QBs will connect with open receivers, or execute an inside handoff to running backs. Fake handoff to one Running Back (RB) and pitch to the other RB who will be able to run or pass. We need to utilize the speed of our running backs. If the QB hands the ball off, he becomes an open receiver.

We will also alternate set up at the line of scrimmage. On one down, receivers and guards will line up on the left side of the Center, on next down, receivers and guards will line up on the right side of the Center, and so on.

We will always keep one wide receiver on the opposite side. This should keep our opponent guessing as to what we are going to do.

New Defensive Strategy

In the next game, we will reverse our defensive coverage. Up to this point, our fast, tall defensive players have played Free Safety and Deep Zone coverage. Monday you will move forward and rush or play Mid-Zone coverage to break up the short pass plays. We will take our chances on our opponent connecting a long bomb, but we have to put pressure on them.

Bat the Ball—Defense, make sure you go after that ball! Whatever it takes, get to the ball and bat it down or intercept it. Don't let that receiver catch the ball!

Pull Flags—Look at the hips of the runner. Grab and pull their flags! Don't tackle them, but grab those flags and don't let go!

Read the Play—Look at how your opponent's offense lines up, and see if you can read the play. Yell out to your team to *watch the run, watch the pass*, etc.

Man-to-Man—Our last line of defense is to run *man-to-man* coverage. Those of you who are playing corner positions, keep your eye on the receivers coming off the line and pick them up man-to-man to break up the plays.

Engage Your Opponent—If you see an opponent line up who you think is going to catch the ball, engage them. Yell out, "I have 15," or whatever the player's number is. Try to scare them or shake them up a little bit.

Be on Purpose—Everything you do: snap the ball, run the ball, pass, receive, block, defend, or pull flags–do with purpose! Set your sites on your objective and don't give up until you have accomplished what you set your mind to.

Game Recap—*The Agony of Defeat*

(Coach Payne)

After 2 games, the Lions have now experienced the thrill of victory and the agony of defeat. Playing their first road game in the Menifee desert, the Lions were bested 36-0 by Santa Rosa Academy's A team–a collection of tall, speedy 7th graders. Despite the outcome and score, there were a number of positive take-aways from today's game.

Throughout the game, the Lions dealt well with adversity, keeping their collective heads up always looking to the next offensive or defensive series and focusing on what they individually could do to improve the team's fortunes.

There were some *themes* we've seen consistently in practice and now through two games—Team Alpha's John Henry connected with Branden Flanagan for over 40 yards. Team Omega's Mitchell Foster to Kobe Daludado continues to be a potent combination. Branden Flanagan was the defensive MVP, making his presence known throughout the game with 2 interceptions and multiple stops.

The Lion's defense had 3 sacks. One each by Kobe and Eldon Meacham, and even a combination sack by Kobe and Caleb Smeraldi! Eldon also had 2 other tackles including a touchdown saving stop down the right sideline late in the 1st quarter. Among names being called for the first time, Daniel MacDonald caught a John Henry pass and broke up a 1-point conversion literally using his head. Taylor Weiss caught his first Mitchell Foster pass.

While it was humbly noted in the post-game prayer that losing can teach us life lessons, the Lions will try to get back into the win column on Monday when they head back to the Menifee Serengeti to battle Santa Rosa Academy's B team.

One way to find out how to do something right is to do it wrong.
- Coach Crume

Santa Rosa "B"

42-0 – Linfield Lions

Game Recap—*Santa Rosa "B"*

(Coach Payne)

What a difference a few days make! The Lions returned to the plains of Menifee avenging Friday's 36-0 loss, beating Santa Rosa Academy's B Team 42-0.

The Lions wasted no time, scoring on their first play from scrimmage when Kobe Daludado took the handoff from quarterback Mitchel Foster, zigzagging 60 yards through Santa Rosa's defense (Kobe easily ran twice that distance if you count east-west yardage!).

On the next series, Mitchel and Kobe covered 60 yards in 2 pass plays for another touchdown and a 12-0 lead. Kobe had another huge game with 130 yards combined (rushing and receiving) scoring 2 touchdowns and even recording a tackle on defense!!

After the Lion defense stopped Santa Rosa's offense, quarterback Mitchel Foster moved the Lions across midfield with a 25-yard completion to Justin Locke. Douglas Pettigrew then burst onto the scene, tearing over the right side of the line and racing 30 yards for the Lions 3rd touchdown (Douglas' first!)

Not to be lost in Team Omega's offensive fireworks was the smothering defense played by Team Alpha. Connor Kostecka put an exclamation point on the first half with an interception/touchdown. Kostecka's juggling circus-catch made the score 24-0.

Teams Alpha and Omega switched places in the second half and on their first play, quarterback John Henry found Connor Kostecka streaking down the left sidelines for a 60-yard touchdown bomb and a 30-0 score.

On the next series, Santa Rosa made its first and only excursion into Lion's territory, moving the ball to the Lion's 10-yard line in 2 plays. Just when it looked like the shutout was in jeopardy, Sonny Gomes rose up in the end zone, picking off a Santa Rosa pass and returning it to the 10-yard line from wence it came! 2 series later, Caleb Smeraldi got into the act with an interception/touchdown of his own, making the score 36-0.

Justin Locke set up the Lion's final score with an interception and return to the 1-yard line. Two plays later, John Henry found Branden Flanagan in the back of the end zone for the Lion's final touchdown and a 42-0 lead.

On the last series of the game, Patrick Payne got his first interception and rumbled down to the Santa Rosa 1-yard line. In all, the defense allowed only 1 first down the entire game intercepting 5 passes, scoring 2 touchdowns and setting the offense up for 2 more.

The Lion's return to the practice field tomorrow sporting a 2-1 record and feeling very good about themselves and their total team victory!

Victory is to be enjoyed not flaunted.
- Coach Crume

Make Life Better

Your mission today, should you chose to accept it, is to Make Someone's Life Better. Today, find ways to do something good for someone; not just anyone, but someone who you normally wouldn't hang around with.

I want you to focus on finding someone who isn't in your click or "popular club" and make life better for them. A simple "high five," carry their books, go out of your way to say hi, take a few minutes asking them how they are doing in school, or maybe even sitting down and eating lunch with them and getting to know them. Make someone's life better today!

Winning On & Off the Field

We must maintain a winning attitude on the field, at home and in the classroom. Make sure you are working on your grades and your relationships and responsibilities at home just as hard, and even harder, than you are working on the football field.

Agility

In practice today we worked on, and will continue to work on, agility. *Agility is the ability to break right and left quickly*, to dart and dodge our opponents, or to think quickly on our feet in the face of pressure.

How *suddenly* you can move in another direction to throw off your defenders, will help you turn defeat into victory, a tackle into a touch down. In Football and Life, you must be quick on your feet and able to dodge your opponent quickly.

Sometimes you only have seconds to make the decision—get in the car or not, take that drink or not, go to the party or not, disobey your parents or not, listen to your instinct or not. Your ability to dodge your opponent and to think clearly and quickly on your feet under pressure will assure you more victories and less defeats, both on and off the field.

WHAT'S THE SCORE?

Our stats show we are 2 & 1, but my score is "0 to 0." Once we get a little victory under us it's easy to "relax" thinking "we got this."

The only thing "we got" is an opportunity to excel in all areas of football and life. And we only "got" a few more weeks of regular season to get that job done. Keep your heads down, and keep giving more! We will celebrate when the season's over.

STAR CHALLENGE

Starting today, we will begin to implement our "Star Challenge." As a team it is our goal that everyone gets their name in the "record book" at least once before the end of the season.

That means everyone carries the ball, receives the ball, makes the interception or TD or makes the "star" defensive play. Each player will pair up with another team member, and it will be your responsibility, at practices and at games, to help one another be their best.

Your Assignment: *Set each other up for success.*

NEW LEVEL—NEW DEVIL

It seems that have been "hit hard" lately with "issues" that have caused some players to miss practice and upcoming games. I understand that there are normal things that prevent players from being at practice or games, like travel schedules and pre-scheduled appointments. But some players have missed games or practice because they have been randomly hurt during the school day or have gotten sick.

We have a saying in ministry, *New Level—New Devil.* In other words, when we decide to go up to the next level in life, in our commitment to God, to do better in school or at our jobs, or decide to live or act according to a Higher Standard, we can sometimes get hit with difficulties that appear "out of nowhere."

But the Bible tells us in **1 Peter 5:8** "Be sober, be vigilant; because your adversary the devil, as a roaring lion, walketh about, seeking whom he may devour."

Some things that we get hit with are normal, but some are a battle on a different level. But even in those battles, we can "Put on our Armor" and find confidence in Ephesians 6:10-18 that instructs us, "Finally, be strong in the Lord and in his mighty power.

I encourage you to your armor on so you can take your stand against the enemy's attacks. Also, take a few extra minutes tonight before you go to bed and ask the Lord's blessing on all of our Players, Coaches, and Families as we continue to pursue excellence in Christ, in Life and on the Football Field.

Mt. Zion

24-18 – Linfield Lions

October 15,

Dear Lions,

I AM SO PROUD OF YOU! Today, AGAIN, everyone stepped up your game. You kept your heads together, supported each other, and even when we got behind, TOGETHER you took back control of the game, which produced winning results.

I want to give a shout out to Mr. Brunell for a great game! Josh, you did an AWESOME job at running the ball, catching the ball and making great plays! Way to go!

A quick shout out to Mr. MacDonald who came ALIVE out there today! Daniel, great receiving the ball today! Great running, great play-making and giving your all!

Great job Mr. Henry for leading the team down the field, even under pressure. John, you managed your emotions, connected with your receivers and advanced the ball - Great Job!

"Hoorah" to my seventh graders—Locke & Flanagan. Way to make some great plays out there and help LEAD your team to victory!!

Mr. "Hands," I mean Mr. Kostecka—great job at receiving and advancing the ball today. You even "took it on the chin" to catch the ball and make big plays. Douglas "Bulldog" Pettigrew way to put PRESSURE on that QB.

Mr. Smeraldi, way to keep the pressure on that corner receiver. Keep believing in yourself!

DEFENSE—you did an AWESOME JOB at putting SOLID pressure on your opponent. A couple times their receivers got behind you and made some great plays, but you came right back and caused them to turn over the ball. You helped save the game. GREAT JOB!

OFFENSE - Way to MOVE THE BALL DOWN FIELD! You thought on your feet and made good, SMART plays. You played well together and were able to make critical plays at critical moments!

Lions, if you don't know this by now, let me remind you of how PROUD I am to be your Coach. Each of you have a place in my heart. Regardless of what position you play, or how many "shout-outs" you get, this team would not be the same without each of you! Each time you are on the field, in practice or in a game, I see you growing!

I Believe In You!

See You on the Field!

~ Coach Crume

GAME RECAP

Game Recap—*Mt. Zion*

(Coach Payne)

After a 2-game road trip, the Lions returned to the friendly confines of their home field, beating an undermanned, but relentless, Mt. Zion Eagles squad 24-18, improving their record to 3-1.

The Lions were without a few of their stars, but John Henry had a fantastic game. Playing quarterback the entire way, John completed 8 passes for 132 yards and 1 touchdown, a 20-yard strike to Branden Flanagan. John was also perfect on 2-point conversions connecting 3 times with Connor Kostecka and Daniel MacDonald.

Perhaps John's biggest play, though, was on defense when he broke up a potential game-tying TD on the Eagles last possession.

Josh Brunell, starting at running back, had a quite a coming out party, leading the team in rushing with 105 yards on 8 carries and providing the winning margin with a 15 yard touchdown sprint down the left sideline late in the second half!

Also turning heads was Daniel MacDonald who was seemingly all over the field Friday! After the Lion's offense stalled on their first 2 possessions, Daniel took matters into his own hands, snatching a Mt. Zion pass away from the intended receiver and dashing 15 yards to the end zone.

Connor Kostecka had a great all-around effort leading the Lions in receiving yardage with 4 catches for 75 yards, 6 yards rushing, 3 tackles, and even returned an interception 20 yards, all while exhibiting a Michael Jordan-esque tongue-wag.

Another all-around star, Branden Flanagan caught 3 passes for 47 yards and a touchdown. On the defensive side, Branden had a tackle and an interception. Justin Locke led the defense with 4 tackles and also intercepted a Mt. Zion point-after conversion attempt.

The Lions will put their perfect home record on the line Monday when they square off with St. Jeanne's at 3:30PM.

St. Jeanne's

40-28 - St. Jeanne's

October 18th

Parents & Players,

I just wanted to encourage the Lions that we played a good strong game! Sure we made some errors, but we still played like champions. The greatest improvement I saw was our self-control! We hardly complained about calls or plays in the entire game, and for that you all get a great big "Hoorah!"

I want to give a big shout-out to Coach Woolsey and the Linfield Lions Cheerleaders for cheering for us on today. I would like to give a *special thank you* to all of the Linfield Faculty whose support today made the game that much more special to us.

Thank you Mr. Kostecka for keeping stats, the Henry family for snack, the Kelley family for the Gatorade, Coach Brunell for his assistance, and ALL OF THE PARENTS who continue to show your support game after game.

Thank you also to everyone who helped set up and tear down. I am SO BLESSED by everyone coming together to make this season the best it can be.

I Believe in You!

See You on the Field!

~ Coach Crume

The Night Before

Thoughts

October 24

Players & Parents,

I pray you had a great weekend. In just a few hours, it will be Monday again. This week will be filled with new opportunities and possibilities disguised as problems and challenges. Here is a verse to help you jump-start your week.

Lamentations 3:22-23—"The steadfast love of the Lord never ceases; his mercies never come to an end, they are new every morning. Great is your faithfulness."

Whether you are headed off to school to learn a new subject, prepare for tests, or study the next chapter in History, or you are off to take on a new project at the office, be encouraged that *the mercies of God never come to an end.* Every new day comes with just the right supply of God's love, mercy and faithfulness to help us succeed in that day.

GAME STRATEGY—*Van Avery*

Van Avery is a very GOOD team, but SO ARE WE! They have artificial turf, so Lions make sure you wear your cleats if you have them, or your best tennis shoes.

We will need to be quick on offense and strong on defense to win against Van Avery. We want to score quickly and get the momentum on our side.

DEFENSE

We need to tighten our defensive corners. We played a great game against St. Jeanne, but they beat our defensive corners.

Defense, remember the *golden rule* "Don't let the receiver get behind you!" We also gave away a lot of yards to St. Jeanne by playing them "too loose." Defense, tighten up, but not too much that the receivers get around you.

RUSHERS

Don't over run the QB. During the St. Jeanne's game, our Rushers put great pressure on the QB, but we over ran them.

Rushers, pick out a stopping point 2-3 yards in front of the QB and rush to that spot and slow down. That way if the QB shifts left or right you will be able to move with him. Remember to get your hands up when you get close to the QB. Do whatever you can to get those flags!!

Also, we will play a *pressure rush*—rushing 2 rushers at the beginning of the game. That means the rest of the defense needs to "beef up" the mid 7-10 coverage.

OFFENSE

Team David will lead the Lions in offense and defense until we get settled in and get some points on the board. Everyone be ready to substitute. Bring your FOCUS, your FAITH, and your FIGHT. This will be a game to remember!

I Believe in You!

See You on the Field!

~ Coach Crume

Even the most well thought-out plans fail sometimes.
- Coach Crume

Van Avery

34-0 – Van Avery

It is Monday evening after the game. I've eaten dinner, settled into my desk chair and I have my Bible in front of me.

Whenever I have a problem I don't know how to solve, I go to God's Word to find an answer. The best thing about God is He has all the answers.

I asked the Lord, under my breath, as I was sitting at my desk, where to go in His Word to find something that I could share with you regarding tonight's game. I was led to the book of Joshua. I would like to quote **Joshua 1:1-9** (New Living)

After the death of Moses the Lord's servant, the Lord spoke to Joshua son of Nun, Moses' assistant. He said, 2 "Moses my servant is dead. Therefore, the time has come for you to lead these people, the Israelites, across the Jordan River into the land I am giving them.

I promise you what I promised Moses: 'Wherever you set foot, you will be on land I have given you. No one will be able to stand against you as long as you live. For I will be with you as I was with Moses. I will not fail you or abandon you.

"Be strong and courageous, for you are the one who will lead these people to possess all the land I swore to their ancestors I would give them. Be strong and very courageous. Be careful to obey all the instructions Moses gave you. Do not deviate from them, turning either to the right or to the left. Then you will be successful in everything you do.

Study this book of instruction continually. Meditate on it day and night so you will be sure to obey everything written in it. Only then will you prosper and succeed in all you do. This is my command, be strong and courageous! Do not be afraid or discouraged. For the Lord your God is with you wherever you go."

The time had come for Joshua to lead God's people into the promise land. Moses died and now it was Joshua's turn. This was a BIG moment for Joshua. Everything that God had told Joshua all his life that one day he would be and do, was now staring him right in the face.

Now, I want you to go back and count how many times God told Joshua to be strong and of a good courage. *How many did you come up with?* Three, right? Let's look at them together.

VERSE 6—"Be strong and courageous."

What's the very next thing God says to Joshua, "For you are the one…"

Linfield Lions, you must know that YOU ARE THE ONES! God believes in you! I believe in you! Your parents believe in you, but the opinion that is going to motivate you the most in your life is the opinion you have of yourself!

YOU MUST BELIEVE IN YOU!

VERSE 7—"Be strong and VERY courageous."

God not only tells Joshua to be strong and courageous, but now He tells him to be strong and **VERY** courageous. Why do you think God had to tell Joshua to be strong and VERY courageous? Because fear hits every one of us.

What if I drop the pass? What if I fumble the ball? What if I fail the test? What if everyone laughs at me?

What if I let down my dad? What if I disappoint my mom? What if no one likes me?

The voice of fear always starts with, "what if." Lions, *be strong and very courageous!* This is your time now! This is your season to play football! We have just a few more games and practices.

We will win games and we will lose games, but from this moment forward we will be *strong* and *very courageous!*

Why, because Coach says so? NO! Why, because the Bible says so? NO! Because that is who you are! It's your nature to be strong. It's your nature to be courageous. You were designed by God to do this!

COME ON LIONS get that down inside you deep! Chew on those words. Meditate on them over and over and let them build faith in you!

The word for courageous is "AW-MATS." It means *to be strong, alert, courageous, brave or bold.* It means *to make firm or assure.*

"AW-MATS" comes from another word, "Hithpael," which means *to be determined, to make oneself alert, to strengthen oneself, confirm oneself, or to persist in.*

God was not just trying to "pump Joshua up" to get him to do what He wanted him to do. God was trying to get Joshua to take on the identity of whom God had made him to be!

You must SEE and BE who you REALLY are!

Each time we are on that field I am NOT trying to just "pump you up!" I'm trying to get you to SEE and BE who God has made you to be!

I don't care if you make a touchdown or not! I don't care if you're the quarterback, the center, the running back or the water boy! God has made you to be strong and courageous. God has put in you the ability to make yourself alert, to strengthen yourself, to be courageous!

What does a Lion do in the face of adversity? **He stands up! ROARS! He fights with everything he has in him!** I ask it of you every time we get on that field, and I ask it of you again—

GIVE ME EVERYTHING YOU'VE GOT!

VERSE 9—"Be strong and courageous! Do not be afraid or discouraged. For the Lord your God is with you wherever you go."

The King James Version of the Bible reads, "Don't be afraid or dismayed." The word "Dismayed" means: "A sudden loss of courage in the face of danger."

Tonight on that field we had a *sudden loss of courage in the face of danger*. Sure their rusher was fast. Sure they were good–we already knew that–but it wasn't the fact that they were good that beat us, it was the fact that we didn't believe we could win.

God told Joshua to be strong and of good courage three times. Joshua needed to hear that God believed in him, but more than that, God needed to know Joshua believed in himself!

Remember: *The strongest force you have in you is BELIEF— both in God and in YOURSELF!*

I charge you, as God did Joshua. *Be strong and of good courage! Be strong and VERY courageous! Be strong and courageous!*

And DO NOT BE AFRAID or lose your courage in the face of danger or defeat! THE LORD YOUR GOD is with you wherever you go!

I believe in you!

See You on the Field!

~ Coach Crume

Game Recap— *Van Avery*

(Coach Payne)

After a 2-game home stand, a rain-out and AstroCamp Camp, the Lions traveled to Van Avery Prep to face the Eagles A-team. Van Avery lived up to their reputation, breaking a very close game wide open in the 2nd half and cruising to a 34-0 victory. Though the Lions' record slipped to 3-3, they fought hard throughout surrendering several touchdowns on jump-ball passes that could have gone either way.

On offense, the Lions racked up 226 yards of total offense but fell just short of cashing their offensive production into points. On the last play of the half, trailing 8-0, Justin Locke caught a John Henry pass and raced 50 yards down to the Eagles 10 yard line as time expired.

Both John and Justin starred for the Lions, playing on both sides of the ball and were seemingly everywhere! Playing quarterback, John connected on 4 passes for 85 yards, caught one ball for 10 yards, recorded 6 tackles on defense, broke up three passes and had an interception which he returned 15 yards (Douglas Pettigrew applied big pressure to the QB on that one!). Not to be outdone, Justin led all receivers with 88 yards on 4 receptions, had 5 tackles, one sack, and one interception and broke up one pass.

Mitchel Foster, playing QB for teams David and Omega was the Lion's leading passer, actually eclipsing John's passing total by 1 yard! Mitchel completed 8 passes for 86 yards and ran once for 5 yards. Caleb Smeraldi caught 2 passes for 30 yards and made a great tackle on defense.

Kobe Daludado rushed for 50 yards on 6 carries and caught 3 of Mitchel's passes for 23 yards (a testament to the Eagles' defense, this was one of the few times Kobe has been held under 100 yards rushing/receiving). Connor Kostecka also contributed on both sides of the ball with a 10-yard reception, a QB sack and broke up an Eagles pass that would have gone for a big gain.

Also getting into the action was Daniel MacDonald recording one tackle and breaking up an Eagles 2-point conversion attempt. Sonny Gomes also made a big tackle and a good thing too, as Sonny has a cousin who plays on the Eagles! Patrick Payne made his first catch of the year, a 10-yarder for a first down midway through the second half.

There is no rest for the weary as the Lions are in action on the road tomorrow at Temecula Prep in beautiful Winchester. This is a late game with all the action starting at 4:30. See you there!

Your beliefs are taking you somewhere,
the questions is, where?
- Coach Crume

FROM "COACH KAMI"

Today's game was a hard one. That team was hard. But guys (and girl), after that first touch down we were defeated. That's how we lost every single game last year. We were already defeated in our minds, and then once the other team scored, we were done. We were defeated in our head. We knew we were going to lose.

So for tomorrow's game, we need to go into it with an open mind and we need to win. We are playing Temecula Prep tomorrow and we have already beaten them once. The last time wasn't easy. It wasn't like the whole game was just given to us. We needed to work for it.

We to all show up on that field tomorrow with our "A" game and a determination to win! See you tomorrow.

Kami

PS—Here are some things I have noticed while watching you all play. Please take it the right way. I want to help. Each game remind yourself what it is that you need to work on.

Sonny—you are doing great. You are always there whenever anyone needs you. Keep up the hard work.

Mitchel—You are a great QB. Believe in yourself and know that you can do it. Remember everything is on purpose.

Caleb—Man Caleb, you are doing great. Great defense and great offense. Just remember to focus and listen for that count.

Kobe—Kobe, you are doing great. Instead of stopping to cut back when you are running with the ball, try to go just straight through all them at top speed.

Douglas—Douglas, you are truly doing good. Get in there, get your hands up and continue putting great pressure on that QB.

Taylor—You are doing great at centering. Remember to get it right to the QB and immediately after you snap the ball, run a 10-yard button hook, turn and look for the pass.

Justin—You're doing great. Keep pulling those flags, and work on getting those interceptions!

Branden—You're doing fine. Remember to get those flags and cover your man.

John—John, you are doing great! I know sometimes you have a "bad day" and then you beat up on yourself, but don't. The whole team looks up to you.

If you beat yourself up inside, you separate yourself from the team and then the team can't trust that you are going to make the right decisions. Stay on top of your game!

Connor—Connor, Connor, Connor. I'm just kidding, you're fine. The only thing is when you are in man-to-man coverage, you need to just watch your man and not the QB.

Eldon—You are putting great pressure on that QB. Remember to stop about two yards before you get to him, and see which way he rolls so you can cover him better.

Daniel—You are doing a great job overall. You are catching the ball and running with it more than ever!

Josh—You are doing good, Josh. You are great when you have the ball and or are rushing. Keep up the good work.

Noah—Great job, Noah. You are always there when coach needs you, whether you are on the field or on the sidelines.

Patrick—Man Patrick, you are running your patterns and advancing the ball. Way to go!

Sam—You are doing good at putting pressure on the QB. Remember to cheer on your team when you are on the sidelines.

*The most important person
to believe in is yourself.*
- Coach Kami

Temecula Prep

30-14 – Temecula Prep

Great job on the field today! I know we got off to a slow start, but we fought back and put points on the board!

Great Job defense! We put good pressure on their quarterback, and played tighter on our corners. A few things got by us, but all in all we played a strong game.

Offense, it took us a while, but we finally opened up and blasted our way down field to put some points on the board. I have to give a shout out to Sonny, with bee sting and all, got the first down and kept on running!—Way to go Sonny.

I could mention everyone's name tonight because you all had your own moments! *Keep up the great work!*

We have one more game in front of us before getting a break. I know I've been hard on you at times, but it's paying off. I'm watching you develop in areas that you can't see right now. Keep your attitudes positive. Keep seeing yourself as the winners you are!

I want to give a special shout out to Caleb who wasn't able to be with us today. Caleb, we sure missed you!

Remember: *How You See Yourself Is How Others Will See You.*

In Numbers 13, Moses sends 12 spies out to spy out the land God gave them. The spies go out, see all of these giants in the land, get scared and run back to Moses, and 10 of the 12 bring back an evil report.

The 10 spies that brought back a bad report saw themselves defeated before they even attempted taking the land that God said they could have. Then, they said, "We were in our sight as grasshoppers, and so we were in their sight."

Always Remember: *How you see yourself is how others see you!*

You project the way you feel about yourself and the way you see yourself. If you see yourself as *a loser*, *a nobody*, or as *someone no one wants to be around*, guess what, that's what everyone is going to see.

However, if you see yourself as a *winner*, as *confident*, and *assured of yourself*, then others are going to see you that same way.

Remember: *Most of what you think people are thinking about you isn't the way they are thinking about you at all!*

ALWAYS keep a positive attitude about yourself!

Tomorrow when we take the field, it's OUR FIELD! This is OUR TURF and we are the LINFIELD LIONS! See yourself victorious before you ever walk on that field. Hold your head up high. Be a force to be reckoned with!

YOU CAN DO THIS!

Branden, Justin, Caleb, Josh, Douglas, Daniel, Taylor, John, Connor, Sonny, Sam, Noah, Kobe, Patrick, Mitchel, Eldon—I AM PROUD OF YOU!

I believe in you!

See You on the Field!

~ Coach Crume

Game Recap—*Temecula Prep*

(Coach Payne)

The Lions continued their 2 game road trip today, playing the Temecula Prep Patriots in the heart of beautiful downtown Winchester. The Lions started their season against the Patriots, winning a close game at home. Like the first game, the home-team advantage held, with the Patriots winning 30-14, despite a furious second-half rally by the Lions who seemed to get stronger as the temperature fell, and the sun set.

For the day, the Lions generated 347 yards of total offense; churning out 242 yards and 14 points in the second half alone! Mitchel Foster led the Lions in passing with 202 yards and 2 touchdowns on 10 completions (he also recorded 5 tackles on defense!).

Mitchel's favorite target was John Henry. The two connected on 4 passes for 117 yards and both of the Lions' touchdowns, including their first score, a spectacular 60-yard catch and run! John also shared time at QB, passing for 38 yards on 4 completions. Oh, by the way, John led the defense with 7 tackles!

Also involved in the aerial assault was Connor Kostecka with 2 catches for 25 yards, Daniel MacDonald with 2 catches for 20 yards, Taylor Weiss with the game's first catch for 5 yards and Branden Flanagan with 1 reception for 20 yards. Branden also recorded a tackle. Justin Locke had his usual fantastic game with 2 catches for 18 yards, 6 tackles and an interception!

Kobe Daludado was the Lions' leading rusher with 74 yards on 4 carries. Temecula Prep changed their entire defensive game plan once they got a taste of Kobe's elusive moves. Kobe also had 2 tackles on defense and harassed the Patriot's QB numerous times.

Josh Brunell rushed 2 times for 22 yards, recorded one tackle and had several QB hurries as well. Speaking of QB harassment, Douglas Pettigrew recorded two sacks on consecutive plays, single-handedly ruining a Patriots drive late in the first half. Patrick Payne also recorded a tackle.

Sonny Gomes had a great game as well. After being stung by a bee during pre-game warm-ups, Sonny rushed once for 10 yards, caught 2 passes for 35 yards, keeping a late second-half drive alive with a big first down, and recorded a tackle on defense. Surprisingly, Sonny declined an offer to make the pre-game bee sting a game-day ritual.

*How you see yourself is
how others see you.*
- Coach Crume

Santa Rosa "B"

24-8 – Linfield Lions

October 27

Dear Lions,

I'm going to be REALLY SHORT! Great Job Tonight! I was SO PROUD of how you ALL played as a team! Everyone is on my shout-out list tonight!

Our prayers are with John Henry as he recovers from his neck sprain. A BIG shout out to all the parents for your awesome support of our game and season!

Thank you to the Woolsey Family for snack, and the Kelley Family for the Gatorade! Coaches for your great calls and support on the sidelines! Thank you to all of our extra sideline "cheer leaders."

I believe in you!

See You on the Field!

~ Coach Crume

Santa Rosa Shout-Outs

The Sequel

Ok! Ok! I just can't let this one go! All season long I've really taken time to recognize and give shout outs to the players who seem to always perform well. But tonight when the entire team makes the headlines, and especially players who normally don't get their name in the headlines, play GREAT FOOTBALL, I decide, of all times, to be SHORT in my e-mail. *"Wus up wit dat?"*

I just couldn't help it. I had to get my computer back out and give shout-outs where they are due! Now, PLEASE be patient with me, and if I forget your exact special play don't get mad or offended, I'm sure Coach Payne will have your details in the stats. But I was REALLY proud of Noah how he led his team offensively in the second half.

Noah, that's the most time you have spent in a game as QB and you did a GREAT JOB! You handled the ball well, you handled yourself well, you connected with your receivers, and you should be very proud of yourself! I know I am. Great Job!

Sonny, you did awesome! You were STRONG on offense and defense! The play where you batted the ball down on defense saving a reception and possible a touchdown, was AWESOME!

Taylor, one of the MOST important positions - CENTER - and you were great at in again tonight! Way to keep your eyes on your QB. And you got in the running action too - WAY TO GO!

Sam, you were "all that and bag of chips!" Great running! Great receiving! Great all around football! I am SO proud of you! You played FOOTBALL tonight son! Great job!

Daniel, you were TOUGH on both offense AND defense! You gave everything you had tonight! Great Job!

Eldon, WOW! What a great job on rushing AGAIN! You and Douglas are *BULLDOG* Rushers!

Douglas, you did a GREAT job today! You did great on both defense and offense! You stayed positive through the whole game, and I REALLY appreciated your prayer at the end of the game too.

Justin, you had another great defensive game, and *Branden*, your CHARACTER shined today! - Hoorah!!

Mitchel, you did a great job at QB in the first half. Way to get us points on the board quickly! Great job calling plays on the fly. Your eyes were on your receivers, and you scrambled well against another fast rusher. You connected passes to Connor that were WAY OUT THERE! And your final reception for the TD–well it speaks for itself.

Patrick, you played great "D" and great "O!" Way to move the ball tonight. I'm proud of you! You played GOOD strong football tonight.

Josh, you were ON tonight again too! I loved the way you ran the ball AND encouraged your team! Way to GIVE YOUR ALL!!

Caleb, WAY TO GO! You played GREAT! Great heads up play on Defense! You GAVE IT YOUR ALL! Thank you!

Connor, GREAT receiving! Great running. And once we got you shoes with some teeth on them, you "tore it up!"

Kobe, GREAT RUNNING! You have a way to slip through the crowd without anyone noticing or being able to catch you!

John Henry, thanks for keeping stats for us and supporting your team from the sidelines today!

Ok, I think I can sleep now. I'm REALLY proud of you guys - you did a GREAT JOB!

You sleep better when
you get things off your chest.
- Coach Crume

Game Recap—*Santa Rosa "B"*

(Coach Payne)

We're not sure if this morning's Santa Ana winds had anything to do with it, but the Lions stayed hot, picking right up where they left off in the second half of yesterday's game, beating Santa Rosa's B Team, 24-8, and improving their record to 4-4 in the last home game of the season.

The Lions' offense compiled 392 yards of scorched earth, easily eclipsing their previous best. Quarterback Mitchel Foster led Linfield to an 18-0 half-time lead with 223 yards passing, including 2 long touchdown bombs of 60 yards each. The first score came on the second series when Mitchel found Connor Kostecka slipping behind the Santa Rosa defense. After the catch, Connor won a furious foot race down the right sideline.

Not leaving anything to chance, Connor handled the 2-point conversion himself, taking a handoff 10 yards around the left side to make the score 8-0. Connor had a fantastic all-around game with 126 receiving yards, 22 yards rushing and recording 3 tackles on defense!

On the very next series, Eldon "Bull" Meacham tackled the Santa Rosa QB in the end zone for a safety and a 10-0 lead. Eldon was just getting started though. Eldon went on to record 2 tackles and even had 10 yards rushing. Taking a cue from Eldon, Douglas "Gloves" Pettigrew set a Lions' record with 3 QB sacks. Nice Hat Trick Douglas!!

Not to be out done, Justin "The Minister of Defense" Locke once again led all Lion defenders with 7 tackles (one touchdown saving stop) and also caught one pass for 10 yards.

Shortly before half-time, Kobe "Who Dat?" Daludado put on a show, hauling in a Mitchel Foster pass then zigging and zagging 60 yards to the end-zone. Kobe reached the century mark again, rushing twice for 15 yards and catching 3 passes for 85 more. Kobe also recorded a tackle for the Lions' swarming defense.

Branden Flanagan hauled in a 10-yard pass from Mitchel for the 2-point conversion and an 18-0 half-time lead. Branden later added another 10-yard reception and recorded 2 tackles!

Noah Woolsey took over at quarterback for the Lions in the second half and completed 4 passes for 90 yards including an eye-popping 60 yard touchdown strike of his own–connecting with Mitchel Foster on the last play of the game. Mitchel's long run after the catch put an exclamation point on the game, making the final score 24-8.

Despite the fireworks from Noah and Mitchel, the Lions committed themselves to the ground game in the second half, pounding the ball for 79 yards on 13 rushing attempts. Josh Brunell carried twice for 15 yards. Patrick Payne carried once, rumbling 10 yards for a first down. Sam Kelley showed his stuff with 9 yards rushing and 12 yards receiving. Way to go Sam!

Sonny, who was still recovering from yesterday's pre-game battle with a bee sting, maintained a strong presence on both offense and defense and found her way into the action when she batted down a pass to save a Santa Rosa touchdown–way to go Sonny!

The Lions return to the practice field tomorrow to digest the highs and lows of the last 3 games. From the sounds on the sidelines, everybody has a few ideas to try out tomorrow. It will be their final practice before next week's final slate of 3 road games.

Final Week

Learn, Practice, Apply

Congratulations Linfield Lions for making it to your final week of regular season football. We have just three games to play in regular season before playoffs.

I'm sure some of you wondered if you would even make the team, let alone to the final week. If you look back, you will see that not only did you make the team, not only did you make it to your final week of the regular season, you achieved a goal!

You set out to be on the football team and you made it! Not only did you make the football team, you have learned a lot! You've learned a lot about football, about life and about yourself.

Football and Life both are about *learning* and *growing*. You can't learn the entire football playbook in a day, and you won't learn the Playbook of Life in a day either, it takes time; in fact a lifetime.

In life, just like in football, you have the opportunity to learn, to practice, and to apply. One day at a time, one experience at a time, one lesson at a time, you grow into the person God has created you to be.

LEARN

To be successful in life you must become a lifelong *learner*; in the classroom and in every area of life. Become a student of life. Read, study, watch, and take in everything around you.

Become an observer of life. Observe life, choices, consequences, good and evil, right and wrong, success and failure. Discover what causes people to succeed and others to fail, and make a conscious effort to learn what causes you to succeed and fail.

Learn to see with more than just your physical eyes. Develop your *inner eyes*. Develop discernment, understanding and wisdom that will help lead and guide you in life. In all your getting, get *understanding*. To become the best you that you can possible be, remember to do the following every day:

PRACTICE

Practice what you learn every day. Don't let one single day in your life go by without practicing. Practice means to do or perform often, or to perform or work at repeatedly so as to become proficient.

Remember: *Everything in life takes practice!*

Football takes practice. The very first pass you catch with your face instead of your hands doesn't mean you don't know how to play football. First, it means you need to learn that in football you use your hands to catch the ball, not your face. Secondly, you learn that you need to practice more.

Could you actually get better at catching a football? Of course you could. If you could get better catching a football, could you get better at Baseball, at Soccer, or maybe Skateboarding? Could you get better at Math or Science? How about speaking in front of your class, or making friends with someone you don't know?

"The very first pass you catch with your face instead of your hands doesn't mean you don't know how to play football."

If you could get better at sports and school, could you get better at Life? How about treating your brother or sister nicely? Could you get better at honoring your Mom and Dad? *Could you actually get better at becoming a better you?*

I will let you discover the answers to those questions, but I assure you that whatever you set your heart and mind to *learn* and *practice* everyday of your life, you will become proficient in. Work harder on yourself than anything else.

APPLY

Life is not just about learning, but *applying* what you've learned. You could know how to save our planet but if you never did anything with what you know, nothing would ever change. You could know how to make someone laugh, but if you never told a joke, no one would ever receive the benefit of what you know how to do.

Remember: *Knowledge isn't power, knowledge applied is power.*

You won't know if what you know works unless you *apply* it. Find a way everyday to apply what you learn. Become a problem solver. Life rewards you for solving problems.

The bigger the problem you can solve, the greater the reward you will receive. Become a Master problem solver and life will reward you well.

In a couple of days we will take the field again. It's my prayer that you take some time this weekend to reflect back on what you've learned so far from the games you've played and practices we've had. Reach down deep and apply yourself even harder than ever before.

Let's make these last three games of the season the best games we have ever played!!

I believe in you!

See You on the Field!

~ Coach Crume

Temecula Charter

18-6 – Temecula Charter

November 1

Dear Lions,

We almost got 'em! We had a several opportunities, but just couldn't seem to convert. We got sure got to see some razzle-dazzle from offense and strong defense again. I think Mitchel gets a trophy for running the most yards behind the line of scrimmage.

We certainly don't want to let our guard down going into tomorrow. We've beat Mt. Zion before, but I'm certain they have improved a lot since we saw them first on our field.

Defense—remember not to let those receivers get behind you or those runners turn the corner on you. **Offense**—let's go back to 7-10-yard passes and runs up the center for yardage. We have to do better at moving the ball offensively tomorrow.

Keep your spirits high! Keep seeing yourself winning! It's not over until it's over!!

I believe in you!

See You on the Field!

~ Coach Crume

NFL's Greatest Comeback

Buffalo Bills' kicker Steve Christie booted a 32-yard field goal through the uprights in overtime on January 3, 1993 to cap the National Football League's greatest comeback.

The 1992 AFC Wild Card game looked to be over before it started. The Houston Oilers quickly built a 28-3 half-time lead with the help of four Warren Moon touchdown passes. What was believed to be the final nail in the coffin came just moments into the second half when Houston strong safety Bubba McDowell intercepted a passed and ran 58 yards for another Oiler score.

Faced with watching their team trail by 32 points, many fans made their way to the parking lot while the Bills headed for the record book. Buffalo's backup quarterback Frank Reich, who was filling in for the injured Jim Kelly, led the charge. Interestingly, Reich who played behind Boomer Esiason in college at Maryland, led the Terrapins to the greatest comeback in college football history as a senior.

Buffalo began their rally with a one-yard run by Kenneth Davis and when Christie recovered the ensuing onside kick, Reich took over the show. He calmly directed the offense as he connected first with Don Beebe and then hooked up with Andre Reed for three more touchdowns. The Bills' flurry put them ahead 38-35 with just under 3 minutes to play. With seconds left in regulation, the Oilers' Al Del Greco tied the score with a 26-yard field goal kick to send the game into overtime.

Early into the extra session, defensive back Nate Odomes intercepted a Moon pass to set the stage for Christie's dramatic finish.

(Source: Pro Football Hall of Fame)

Game Recap—*Temecula Charter*

(Coach Payne)

The Lions entered the home stretch of the season with the first of 3 road games, dropping a very tough game to the Temecula Charter Cougars 18-6. The Lions seemed poised to take control of the game on 3 trips deep into Cougar territory but couldn't cash in, and a very close game slipped away as time expired.

Despite the Lions having 7 plays of more than 20 yards, this was primarily a defensive struggle. Temecula Prep served up a steady diet of counter plays, continually running misdirection to the weak side, hoping to isolate their speedy running back on 1 or 2 defenders. The Lions defense, however, wasn't fooled. Seventh graders Justin Locke and Branden Flanagan led the effort, combining for 10 tackles (5 each).

Several times Justin and Branden made open-field touchdown-saving tackles. Justin also had a tackle for a loss and stopped a 2-point conversion attempt. John Henry and Daniel MacDonald each had 2 big tackles. Eldon Meacham, Douglas Pettigrew, Mitchel Foster and Connor Kostecka all recorded tackles as well.

The Lions' offense moved the ball on big plays but struggled to find consistency. Despite bogging down several times inside the 10-yard line, there were numerous highlights. On the second series of the game Kobe Daludado answered a Cougars' touchdown, snagging a long Mitchel Foster pass at the 30 yard line and kicking in the after-burners down the left sideline to tie the game at 6-6.

On the day, Mitchel completed 5 passes for 133 yards and gained another 35 on his only rushing attempt! Kobe added 35 yards rushing on 3 attempts, for 95 combined yards!

Several receivers had big catches. Connor Kostecka had 2 grabs for 33 yards, Sonny Gomes had a spectacular 28-yard catch and run on John Henry's only pass of the day. John also caught a pass for 15 yards.

Perhaps the highlight of the day though was a flea-flicker whereby Kobe took the snap, pitching to Mitchel who ran sideline to sideline 3 times eluding 2 Cougar rushers time and again before heaving a 25-yarder to Branden Flanagan. If the Lions ever need to eat a few minutes of clock, they should dial that one up again!

The road trip continues tomorrow with an excursion into San Diego County and a showdown with Mt. Zion in Fallbrook. The Lions will be trying to even their record at 5-5, giving themselves a chance at a winning record heading into the playoffs.

Difficult is only a
matter of perspective.
- Coach Crume

Mt. Zion

30-20 – Linfield Lions

November 2

Dear Lions,

You should all be in bed by now—hint, hint. I wanted to give a shout out to everyone tonight for playing a great game and for a great win!

I felt we "gelled" more tonight as a team than we have in the last several games. I also want to congratulate everyone on your sportsmanship under very difficult conditions. I encourage you to maintain that attitude of sportsmanship even on campus tomorrow as you share your win with your friends.

Connor, Daniel and John—way to "take the big hits" and get back on your feet. More importantly, thank you for not letting what happened to you on the "outside" get on the "inside." You took some pretty hard shots, yet you held your tongue, bounced back, and played great football!

Noah—great job in the QB slot and great reception and TD. Josh had a knock down. Connor tip-toed into the end zone, Justin and Branden were strong on defense. Taylor got in there tonight with a reception. Sonny got her hands on the ball. Kobe navigated the field for points. Mitchel helped the offense move the ball. Great teamwork between Noah, John & Mitchel.

I don't have the "write up" so I can't give you all the details. If I missed a name or two please forgive me. Defense you were very strong again tonight! I wish I could have captured John Henry's fingertip interception on video. John, I think you grew three inches on that pick–great job!

Balls were being intercepted and batted down. Sacks were happening, we were moving the football and putting up points! I appreciated the team spirit on the sidelines, even the players who didn't get a lot of game time tonight were very supportive.

I wanted to draw attention to the defense. If you are on defense, you are a VERY IMPORTANT player on this team. I know offense seems to "get the glamour" a lot of the times, but we would have not won tonight if the defense was not as strong as you were. So "Hoorah" to defense.

Also, please know that I'm trying my best to get everyone game time. You ALL contribute SO MUCH to this team. At times I may go to a few of our stronger players to put up some points, or shut down our opponent's offense, but that does not diminish anyone's value on this team.

EACH OF YOU MAKES ALL OF US SUCCEED!

I believe in you!

See You on the Field!

~ Coach Crume

*Great character is revealed
under great pressure.*
- Coach Crume

St. Jeanne's

6-6 – Tie

Game Recap—*St. Jeanne's*

(Coach Payne)

The Lions wrapped up their 3 game road trip and their regular season Wednesday coming from behind to tie St. Jeanne's 6-6. The tie gives the gives the Lions a 5-5-1 mark for the regular season.

The Lions moved the ball well at times Wednesday combining for 209 yards of total offense but struggled with consistency inside the red zone. Behind 6-0, midway through the 2nd half, Linfield scored their lone touchdown on a 25-yard catch by Daniel MacDonald. Daniel caught a short pass from John Henry then did the rest himself, eluding the entire Saint Jeanne's defense while spinning and juking down the right sideline! It was just an outstanding individual effort!

On the day, QB Mitchel Foster completed 4 passes for 47 yards and John Henry, also playing QB, added another 62 yards on 5 completions. Mitchel also ran the ball well, rushing twice for 30 yards. John contributed 10 yards on 2 carries. Both had great all around games with John making significant contributions on defense as well, recording 4 tackles, an interception and a tipped pass.

Kobe Daludado again led all Lions rushers with 43 yards on 5 attempts. Kobe also had a catch for 15 yards and a first down. Kobe was unleashed on defense in the second half recording one sack and hurrying the Saint Jeanne's QB several times. The Lions generated significant QB pressure all afternoon with Douglas Pettigrew, Connor Kostecka, Caleb Smeraldi, Josh Brunell and Justin Locke all bringing the heat (*these guys would make coffee nervous*)!

The deuces were wild with Daniel, Josh, Branden Flanagan and Connor who all recorded 2 tackles apiece. Justin Locke again led all defenders with 5 tackles, including one for a 5-yard loss. Sure-handed Sonny Gomes and Eldon Meacham also made clutch contributions with Sonny making a crucial first down on a 12-yard reception and Eldon catching 2 balls for 15 yards.

The Lions seemingly saved their best for the very last though. With 5 seconds left and the ball on their own 10-yard line, John Henry threw a short pass to Branden Flanagan. With three defenders surrounding him and seemingly nowhere to go, Branden alertly lateralled back to John who seized the opportunity, knifing through the heart of the St. Jeanne's defense, sprinting 50 yards to glory and what appeared to be the winning touchdown.

But alas, the referee, while expressing considerable admiration for the play, asked for an interpretation of the rules having never seen anything quite like it. Coach Crume went through the rule book and found, near the very end, on line 31, it clearly stated that a player was not allowed to lateral the ball beyond the line of scrimmage.

The Lions may have lost a touchdown and tied the game but *learned a valuable lesson in ethics and integrity*. That said, it was an amazing play and great inspiration as Linfield prepares for the playoffs, which begin week after next.

All things are possible to him who believes.
- Jesus

LifeSeeds

Seed of Authority

Sooner or later you must learn to yield your life to *authority*. Authority is the power to influence or command thought, opinion, or behavior. Develop a healthy honor and respect for all authority—*Public Authority*, *Spiritual Authority*, and *Personal Authority*.

PUBLIC AUTHORITY

Public Authority includes school teachers, police officers, managers, coaches, team captains, the President of the United States—anyone who you report to for a certain amount of time during the day or for a certain function, or who enforce rules and regulations that govern your life in one way or another.

SPIRITUAL AUTHORITY

Spiritual Authority includes your Pastor, Priest, Rabbi, Sunday School Teacher, Youth Leader, Bible Study Teacher—anyone who speaks into your life spiritually.

PERSONAL AUTHORITY

Personal Authority includes your parents, step-parents, older siblings, uncles, aunts—anyone who is related to you that are your elders.

I realize that when you are growing up, *Authority* seems more like control. It seems like people in authority just get a kick out of telling you what to do all the time. And for some people in authority who have issues with control, that's true.

Some people in authority make themselves feel good by making other's feel bad, or make themselves feel big by making others feel small. But *true authority doesn't destroy, it develops*. True authority doesn't confine, it refines and releases. There is no greater force on the planet than authority in love.

True authority is necessary for your personal growth and development. Be careful not to develop resentment toward authority. You need authority in your life to lead and guide you, to keep you safe, and to see that you reach your destiny.

Your coach is a person in authority, your teacher is a person in authority, your parents are people in authority, the police officer is a person in authority, and the President of the United States is a person in authority.

The law of our country are also a form of authority in your life. So is your a student code of conduct handbook. ***Rules and regulations that govern your life in one way or another are Authority.***

I look at Authority in two different categories: ***Verbal Authority*** and ***Written Authority***.

Verbal Authority—*People*

The first category of authority is *Verbal Authority* or *people who are in authority over you.* For example your mom or dad, teachers, police officers, your coach, or your boss at work.

How you respond to people who are in authority over you, how you learn to respect them, honor them, and follow their instruction, will determine how fast you grow; or even if you grow into the person you've been created to be.

LifeSeed: *Obedience is the key that unlocks greatness in you.*

Written Authority—Law/Instruction

The second category of authority is what I call "Written Authority," or "Law or Instruction." The Laws of our Country would be an example of written authority. The Student Code of Conduct for your school is an example of *written authority*.

The sign in the parking lot that says, "Put Carts Here" is an example of written authority. The difference with written authority is there is no one there to enforce it. It's totally up to you whether you will follow it or not.

You see, if the teacher is standing over you telling you that you are going to finish your homework or else, you feel the pressure of his or her authority. If mom or dad is watching over your shoulder while you are surfing the Internet, you feel the pressure of authority and are "forced" or "obligated" to obey their rules.

If you see a police officer, whether you are doing anything wrong or not, there is pressure to make sure you are obeying the law so you don't get a ticket. But that pressure comes from the outside. *Following authority when no one is looking requires pressure from your inside, or conviction.*

CONVICTION—Conviction is a strong persuasion or belief. Conviction is the pressure of authority in the absence of physical authority.

You know Mom and Dad said they don't want you listening to music with fowl language in it, but Mom and Day are not around, so what do you do? You are at a friend's house and they start to watch a movie that you know you don't watch in your home, what do you do? You feel the pressure of authority inside you, but no one is around.

LifeSeed: *What you do when no one is looking will determine whom you will be when everyone is looking.*

Eventually who you really are comes to the surface. You can't hide anything. Sooner or later everything you do will be exposed for all to see. *Train yourself to do what's right when no one is looking;* you will reach your destiny a lot faster.

LifeSeed: *You can't be in authority until you have learned how to be under authority.*

Being under authority doesn't mean you're weak, it means you're strong. It takes a confident, strong person to submit him or herself to someone else's authority. Someone will always be over you. The key is to trust the authority that is over you.

Trusting Authority

In order for you to grow to your full potential, you are going to have to trust someone in authority. You have to find a Parent, a Teacher, a Pastor, Priest, Businessperson, Sibling, Mentor or Coach—someone you trust with your future. You must give that person permission to "sow into your life" and you must receive what they are sowing.

You are letting someone to influence you, the question is who? Who are you allowing to influence you?

LifeSeed: *The authority you trust is the authority you allow to influence you.*

Trust is a LifeSeed all of its own, but you must learn to trust someone. Trust is the highest form of honor. Violation of trust is the highest form of dishonor.

If you give your word keep it. Become trustworthy; you will reach your destiny much faster.

LifeSeed: *The greatest demonstration of trust is enduring discipline or correction. The greatest demonstration of love–true love–is administering discipline or correction.*

Endure Chastising—*Hebrews 12:5-13*

5 And you have forgotten that word of encouragement that addresses you as sons: "My son, do not make light of the Lord's discipline, and do not lose heart when he rebukes you, 6 because the Lord disciplines those he loves, and he punishes everyone he accepts as a son."

7 Endure hardship as discipline; God is treating you as sons. For what son is not disciplined by his father? 8 If you are not disciplined (and everyone undergoes discipline), then you are illegitimate children and not true sons.

9 Moreover, we have all had human fathers who disciplined us and we respected them for it. How much more should we submit to the Father of our spirits and live! 10 Our fathers disciplined us for a little while as they thought best; but God disciplines us for our good, that we may share in his holiness.

11 No discipline seems pleasant at the time, but painful. Later on, however, it produces a harvest of righteousness and peace for those who have been trained by it. 12 Therefore, strengthen your feeble arms and weak knees. 13 "Make level paths for your feet," so that the lame may not be disabled, but rather healed.

There is no higher honor that being a *Son*. Being a Son means you have a Father, being a Father means you have a Son. The Bible says the Lord disciplines those He loves, and punishes everyone he accepts as a *Son*.

Don't misunderstand the term Son with the male gender. *Sonship is about relationship*. The principle of Sonship is just as easily applied to a Daughter or female gender.

One of the ways you recognize a true father is, *a true father disciplines with love*. I didn't just say disciplines, I said disciplines in love. Authentic, genuine, authority disciplines you **and** loves you. In fact, it hurts a true father more to discipline his son than it does the son who is being disciplined.

The greatest pain a father can endure is the pain of disciplining his very own son. But if he doesn't discipline his son, he is not really a son at all.

Hebrews 12:8 says, "If you are not disciplined (and everyone undergoes discipline), then you are *illegitimate children* and not true sons." Discipline without love destroys, but discipline with love develops. You cannot reach your full potential without the right combination of discipline and love.

REJECTION

The second greatest pain of a real father, is the pain of *rejection* of his love and discipline from his very own son.

Rejection isn't just when a girl or guy turns you down to go to the dance, or when someone doesn't want to be your friend. Rejecting Truth, and authentic love and discipline can be devastating to everyone involved.

When you reject what people who love you are sowing into you, you are damaging your life and future beyond what you can see.

LifeSeed: *The most dangerous form of rejection, is the rejection of Truth.*

When someone in your life, who is in authority over you, takes the time to discipline you or bring correction to you with love, WAKE UP and pay attention; it's a sign that he or she truly loves you.

ABUSE

I know we live in a world full of *abuse*. Every second of every day people in authority—*public, spiritual* and *personal*—are using their authority to destroy rather than discipline and love.

But I encourage you, that if you have been abused by someone who should have loved you, go to your Heavenly Father and let Him love you and put the pieces of your life back together again *so you don't become what's happened to you.*

Let go so you can grow.
- Coach Crume

Y ou were never created to be beaten or abused. You were never designed to be destroyed or belittled. You were created to be loved, disciplined and molded and shaped into being everything you can be.

In life, some of us don't get dealt the same hand that others do. Some come from brokenness, rejection, despair, and pain. Some live their lives day in and day out in verbal and physical abuse, and it seems like life will never get better.

I have Good News for you! *For God so loved you that He gave His only begotten Son that whosoever shall believe in Him shall not perish but have everlasting life.*

There is a Father who loves you. There is One who understands you and knows and loves you. ***There is A Love that goes beyond the love of even the greatest father on earth***, and that is the love of your Heavenly Father.

Your Heavenly Father can restore your brokenness. He can put the pieces of your life back together again and cause your future to be bright and full of hope!

If you are one of millions who may have experienced abuse or rejection from someone who should have loved you, I encourage you to *give them to the Lord*.

LifeSeed: *Don't allow yourself to become what someone's done to you or said about you.*

Don't Hate—Don't allow bitterness to form in your heart. Don't allow yourself to become what someone's done to you or said about you. Take back control. Forgive them, for they know not what they have done.

Matthew 11:28—*Come unto me, all ye that labour and are heavy laden , and I will give you rest.*

Forgiveness is your greatest defense.
- Coach Crume

The Playoffs

Temecula Charter
25-22 - Lions

Dear Lions,

Congratulations on a FANTASTIC game tonight! I was so proud of the way you ALL came together and played, by far, THE MOST exciting comeback game, and football, you have played all season! I know a lot of accolades came my way tonight for the win, but Lions, I didn't win that game YOU DID!

Great job to the DEFENSE who SHUT DOWN that double reverse and put points of your own on the board with 2 safeties. Great job to the OFFENSE who MOVED the ball down field and put points on the board, and came through right when we needed it the most.

You ALL deserve a big HOORAH!

I also want to point out that we saw the principle of "Reaping and Sowing" at work tonight on that field. All season long we have played with our "heads held high!" We've taken a lot of "difficult calls" and kept moving forward with the minimal amount of complaining.

Well tonight, I believe we saw the ROI (Return on Investment). Tonight, a couple of times, the decision was in our favor which helped move us into victory. *It does pay to do what's right!*

Tomorrow we go up against Santa Rosa's "A" team. We know who Santa Rosa is, but Santa Rosa doesn't know who we are; at least not the Lions that played on that field tonight.

Get your Faith on! Get your Fight on! See Yourself Winning!

I believe in you!

See You on the field!

~ Coach Crume

Game Recap—*Temecula Charter*

(Coach Payne)

The Lions won their first playoff game *coming from behind* in a hostile road environment to beat the Temecula Charter Cougars 25-22. Having played the Cougars before, the Lions knew they'd be served a steady diet of misdirection running plays and have difficulty stopping the Cougars star running back.

Early in the 4th quarter, it looked as though history might repeat itself as the Lions found themselves on the short end of a 22-8 score. With darkness encroaching and the sun seemingly setting on the Lions season, they staged a furious rally in the final minutes, scoring 17 unanswered points.

With 50 seconds left, Kobe Daludado gave the Lions their first lead of the day, scampering 55 yards to the end-zone. In all Kobe was at his *Who Dat?* best, contributing 115 rushing and receiving yards, and scoring 2 touchdowns in addition to running for a 2 point conversion.

The game was not over, however, until Justin Locke made a season-saving tackle on the game's final play stopping the Cougars' running back's desperate charge through the Lion's defense.

It was appropriate that Justin's tackle sealed the win as the 4 points he scored off of 2 safeties kept the Lions in the game until their offense found its groove. In addition to his 2 safeties, the "Minister of Defense" led all Linfield defenders with 8 tackles.

Also in the spotlight was Mitchel Foster who posed a triple threat, running for 37 yards, throwing for 67 yards and a touchdown—oh, and by the way, catching 3 passes for 42 yards.

John "The Hammer" Henry also had a fantastic game. Playing through a leg injury, John contributed significantly on offense and defense, recording 3 tackles and leading the team in passing with 6 completions for 93 yards and a touchdown.

Another 2-way star was Branden Flanagan, who caught 2 passes for 41 yards and a touchdown, made 3 critical tackles on defense and converted an extra point.

Connor Kostecka made 2 clutch grabs for 42 yards and had 2 tackles on defense. Connor's main contribution though was on defense where he was assigned to shadow the Cougars' star running back. No matter what the play was, "Stick-em" was asked stay with #6 wherever he went. Connor played his man so close that by the end of the game he could tell what kind of gum #6 was chewing!

While there were numerous outstanding individual efforts, this was a complete team effort. Sonny Gomes had a huge 10 yard run and Taylor Weiss had a crucial 10 yard reception to keep a first-half drive alive.

Noah Woolsey had a big tackle and Caleb "Shoelace" Smeraldi was everywhere on defense, sacking the quarterback once, making 2 tackles and wreaking general havoc throughout the game.

Making significant contributions in support on both sides of the ball were Josh "JB" Brunell, Douglas "Dougy Fresh" Pettigrew, Eldon "Bull" Meacham, Patrick "Master P" Payne, Sam Kelley and Daniel MacDonald.

As the Lions advance in the playoff bracket, things don't get any easier tomorrow as the Lions head to arid Menifee to face the goliath of the league, the infamous Santa Rosa "A" team.

It is worth noting that Coach Crume has prepared for just such an occasion, designating a special squad as "Team David" specifically to do battle with giants.

*The next best thing to winning
is coming from behind to do it.*
- Coach Crume

The Playoffs

Santa Rosa A
14-0 - Santa Rosa

Dear Linfield Lions,

Congratulations on a GREAT season! I know today brought a close to your football season, but I'm believing it also brought an opening to a "new you" and a new future!!

I am SO VERY PROUD of all of you, the way you played on the field today. I'm especially proud of all the players who supported your team from the sidelines. Those of you who didn't get the opportunity to play much today, sure showed team spirit by cheering until the very end—*THANK YOU!*

Today proved to be yet another learning opportunity for Coach, (learning never ends), as I dealt with Referees and difficult calls. I must admit, I've grown pretty close to all of you, and I've watched all season long as you have "taken it on the chin" many times to your loss.

Tonight I felt that you more than deserved someone to "go to bat for you!" Despite the challenges, you overcame AGAIN to prove to yourselves that you are a GREAT football team.

You didn't win...but YOU ARE WINNERS!

I look forward to our season celebration where we can all celebrate and share together–and eat those ice cream sundays I promised.

I did want to say a special "thank you" again to all of the parents, grand parents, and families for your terrific support this season. Thank you for helping make this season EXTRA SPECIAL. Driving kids to games, bringing snack, helping set up and tear down, praying for the team, and your presence on the sidelines cheering us on has made the season the BEST!

Thank you also for your understanding and patience with the Coaches. It certainly has been our goal and desire to see that every player got a chance to play and a chance to grow.

Thank you to Coach Woolsey, and the Linfield Lion Cheerleaders for your GREAT support. You always make us feel Extra Special! Thank you to Dan Brunell and Gary Payne for your AWESOME support, mentoring, friendship and help on and off the field. I couldn't have asked for two better Men to help lead us this season - THANK YOU!

Lions, get some rest! Again, I am SO PROUD OF YOU!

I Believe in You!

See You on the Field!

~ Coach Crume

I Believe In You!
- Coach

Honor & Privilege

November 21,

Dear Linfield Lion,

It has been my honor and privilege to be your coach this year. This has been, by far, one of the greatest years of my life; one I will never forget.

I pray that you have discovered, and will continue to discover, the great potential that lies within you. I pray that you have become determined, and will continue to be determined, to believe in yourself and commit your life to becoming all that God has created you to be.

Thank you for being a part of the Linfield Christian Middle School Flag Football team. Your hard work and dedication have paid off. The same dedication and hard work you have exhibited on and off the field this season, will now be required the rest of your life. The score is zero to zero, go for it!

I believe in you!

See You on the Field...of Life!

~ Coach Crume
Volunteer Coach, Flag Football, 2010
Linfield Christian Middle School

Special Thanks

I would like to extend a special thanks to John Broussard, Athletics Director for Linfield Christian Middle School, for giving me the awesome opportunity to coach Middle School Flag Football this year.

I would like to thank Dan Brunell and Gary Payne for being two of the greatest assistant coaches a coach could ever ask for. Thanks for your friendship and for your spirit of excellence, both on and off the field.

I would especially like to thank you parents for entrusting me with you your sons and daughters this season, and for giving me the privilege and honor of sowing seeds of greatness into their lives.

I would also like to thank you; the one reading this book. Even though this book was written primarily to the players and parents of my football team, it's my prayer that the lessons and principles of life I've shared will be inspiring and life changing for you, and that you will grow to be all who God has created you to be, and that you find and fulfill your Divine Destiny.

I pray the LORD bless you and keep you, the LORD make his face to shine upon you, and be gracious to you, the LORD lift up his countenance upon you, and give you hope, prosperity and peace.

In His Service,

Jeff Crume

Picture Memories

LION

P
R
I
D
E

Moments...

create memories...

Linfield Lions

Flag Football
2010

Linfield Lions

#1   Kobe Daludado
#4   Josh Brunell
#6   Douglas Pettigrew
#7   Connor Kostecka
#14 Justin Locke
#17 Branden Flanagan
#18 Caleb Smeraldi
#20 Noah Woolsey
#22 Eldon Meacham
#23 Sonny Gomes
#26 Mitchel Foster
#29 Sam Kelley
#31 Taylor Weiss
#40 John Henry
#41 Daniel MacDonald
#42 Patrick Payne

Flag Football

2010

Season Record
Unofficial
5-5-1
League
3-5-1

Playoff Record
1-1

To invite Jeff to speak at your next School,
Church or Business event, contact:
Jeff Crume Ministries
info@jeffcrumeministries.org

www.ingramcontent.com/pod-product-compliance
Lightning Source LLC
Chambersburg PA
CBHW031318040426
42443CB00005B/127